The ★ ★
UNITED
STATES
PRESIDENTS

Millard

FILLMORE

Heidi M.D. Elston

Big Buddy Books
An Imprint of Abdo Publishing
abdopublishing.com

abdopublishing.com

Published by Abdo Publishing, a division of ABDO, PO Box 398166, Minneapolis, Minnesota 55439. Copyright © 2017 by Abdo Consulting Group, Inc. International copyrights reserved in all countries. No part of this book may be reproduced in any form without written permission from the publisher. Big Buddy Books™ is a trademark and logo of Abdo Publishing.

Printed in the United States of America, North Mankato, Minnesota
062016
092016

THIS BOOK CONTAINS
RECYCLED MATERIALS

Design: Sarah DeYoung, Mighty Media, Inc.
Production: Mighty Media, Inc.
Editor: Rebecca Felix
Cover Photograph: Alamy
Interior Photographs: Alamy (pp. 7, 11, 17, 19, 27, 29); American Political History (pp. 5, 15, 25);
    Corbis (p. 13); Getty (6, 9); Northwind (p. 21); Picture History (p. 23)

Cataloging-in-Publication Data

Names: Elston, Heidi M.D., author.
Title: Millard Fillmore / by Heidi M.D. Elston.
Description: Minneapolis, MN : Abdo Publishing, [2017] | Series: United States
    presidents | Includes bibliographical references and index.
Identifiers: LCCN 2015957281 | ISBN 9781680780925 (lib. bdg.) |
    ISBN 9781680775129 (ebook)
Subjects: LCSH: Fillmore, Millard, 1800-1874--Juvenile literature. |Presidents--
    United States--Biography--Juvenile literature. | United States--Politics and
    government--1850-1853--Juvenile literature.
Classification: DDC 973.6/4092 [B]--dc23
LC record available at http://lccn.loc.gov/2015957281

Contents

Millard Fillmore

Millard Fillmore was the thirteenth US president. He led the country during one of the worst times in American history. The North and the South argued about slavery. Later, these arguments led to the **American Civil War**.

As president, Fillmore helped pass the **Compromise** of 1850. He thought it would solve the country's slavery problems. Fillmore did what he thought was right for the country. He actively served his community and country throughout his life.

Timeline

1800

On January 7, Millard Fillmore was born in Cayuga County, New York.

1847

Fillmore was elected the state comptroller of New York.

1832

Fillmore was elected to the US House of **Representatives**.

1849

On March 5, Fillmore became vice president.

1850

President Zachary Taylor died on July 9. On July 10, Fillmore became the thirteenth US president.

1874

On March 8, Millard Fillmore died.

1853

On March 4, Fillmore left the White House.

Young Millard

Millard Fillmore was born in Cayuga County, New York, on January 7, 1800. He had three sisters and five brothers.

At age 19, Millard moved to Buffalo, New York. He worked in a law office. He soon became a **lawyer**.

★ FAST FACTS ★

Born: January 7, 1800

Wives: Abigail Powers (1798–1853), Caroline Carmichael McIntosh (1813–1881)

Children: two

Political Party: Whig

Age at Inauguration: 50

Years Served: 1850–1853

Vice President: None

Died: March 8, 1874, age 74

Millard's boyhood home

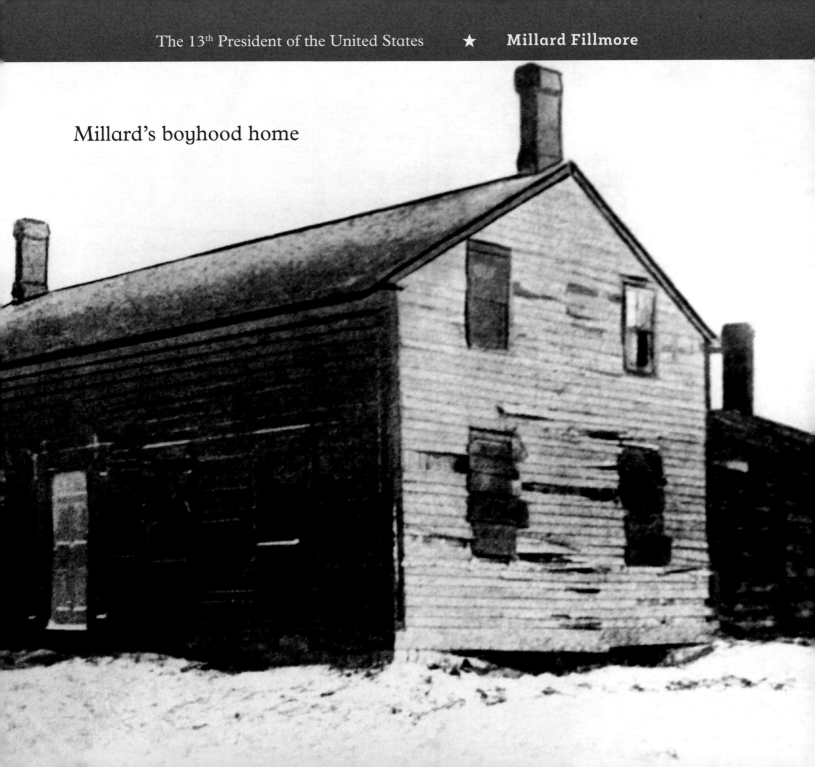

Family and Politics

On February 5, 1826, Fillmore married Abigail Powers. The Fillmores raised two children. Millard Powers was born in 1828. Mary Abigail followed in 1832.

Also in 1828, Fillmore began working in **politics**. That year, he was elected to the New York state **legislature**. At that time, people who could not pay their **debts** were often

Abigail Fillmore was well educated and loved to read. From the time she was 16 years old, Abigail taught school.

put in prison. Fillmore worked to pass laws stopping this punishment for **debt**. The citizens of New York were happy with Fillmore's actions.

In 1832, Fillmore was elected to the US House of **Representatives**. He served in Congress from 1833 to 1835. He served again from 1837 to 1843. In 1834, Fillmore joined the **Whig Party**.

As a congressman, Fillmore **supported** new inventions and businesses. He helped provide inventor Samuel F.B. Morse with money to create the **telegraph**. This invention helped Americans communicate over long distances.

Fillmore became a representative while Andrew Jackson was president. He supported the Whig Party's strong opposition to Jackson.

Nominations

Fillmore ran for governor of New York in 1844. He lost a close election. Fillmore then returned to his law practice. But, he did not give up on **politics**. In 1847, Fillmore was elected the state comptroller. In this position, he handled New York's money.

In 1848, the **Whig Party** chose Zachary Taylor to run for president. Fillmore was named his **running mate**. Taylor and Fillmore won the election! Fillmore became vice president of the United States.

Taylor and
Fillmore's
campaign
poster

Vice President

Fillmore became vice president on March 5, 1849. His main duty was to govern the US Senate. In 1850, the Senate discussed a set of **resolutions** meant to end arguments about slavery.

The resolutions became known as the **Compromise** of 1850. But Taylor was against the compromise. So he would not pass it. Then everything changed. Zachary Taylor died on July 9, 1850. By law, Vice President Fillmore became president.

Fillmore and Taylor came from very different backgrounds. They found they did not agree on much.

Compromise

As president, Fillmore **supported** the **Compromise** of 1850. It said California was a free state. It also said runaway slaves could be returned to their masters.

Fillmore felt a war would start between pro-slavery and antislavery groups without these laws. Congress passed the compromise. Fillmore was sure the slavery problem was solved.

SUPREME COURT APPOINTMENTS

Benjamin R. Curtis: 1851

Kentucky senator Henry Clay proposed the ideas that led to the Compromise of 1850. Many people hoped the compromise would solve the slavery problem.

President Fillmore

President Fillmore also worked for trading rights with other countries. He sent Commodore Matthew Perry on a trip to Japan. This led to the **Treaty** of Kanagawa in 1854. This treaty opened Japanese ports to US ships.

However, Fillmore spent most of his time in office dealing with the slavery problem. The **Compromise** of 1850 was not working. Americans still fought over slavery. Often, antislavery Northerners felt the president was siding with pro-slavery Southerners.

Commodore
Matthew Perry

President Fillmore was caught between the North and the South. Neither side was happy with him. His popularity fell.

Fillmore believed the **Compromise** of 1850 would keep the United States together. Instead, it was pulling the country apart. By 1861, 11 states would leave the United States to form their own country.

★ DID YOU KNOW? ★

In 1855, Oxford University in Oxford, England, offered Fillmore an honorary **degree**. He refused it. The degree was written in Latin, which Fillmore couldn't read.

PRESIDENT FILLMORE'S CABINET

July 10, 1850–March 4, 1853

★ **STATE:** Daniel Webster,
Edward Everett (from November 6, 1852)

★ **TREASURY:** Thomas Corwin

★ **WAR:** George Washington Crawford,
Charles Magill Conrad (from August 15, 1850)

★ **NAVY:** William Alexander Graham,
John P. Kennedy (from July 26, 1852)

★ **ATTORNEY GENERAL:** Reverdy Johnson,
John J. Crittenden (from August 14, 1850)

★ **INTERIOR:** Thomas Ewing,
T.M.T. McKennan (from August 15, 1850),
Alexander H.H. Stuart (from September 16, 1850)

Sad Times

Fillmore was not **nominated** to run for president in 1852. Franklin Pierce was elected president. On March 4, 1853, Fillmore left the White House. He returned to Buffalo and his law practice. Meanwhile, Abigail Fillmore had fallen ill. She died later that month.

Fillmore was greatly saddened by the death of his wife. Just one year later, Fillmore's daughter, Mary, died suddenly. Fillmore was heartbroken. To keep busy, he thought he might return to work in **politics**.

Franklin Pierce
served as president
from 1853 to 1857.

Know-Nothings

The United States and its **politics** were changing. Between the mid-1840s and the mid-1850s, nearly 3 million people **immigrated** to the United States. Many US-born citizens felt the immigrants were a **threat**.

In response, a secret group called the Know-Nothings formed. Its members wanted to pass laws against these newcomers. Soon, the Know-Nothings created a new political party. It was called the American Party. But the party did not last long. It fell apart after 1856.

Fillmore did not agree with the American Party's anti-immigrant message.

Return to Buffalo

Fillmore decided to run for president again in 1856. He lost the election. After this loss, he moved to Buffalo and left **politics** for good.

In Buffalo, Fillmore **supported** the city's libraries. He helped start the Buffalo General Hospital. In 1858, Fillmore married Caroline Carmichael McIntosh.

On March 8, 1874, Millard Fillmore died after suffering two **strokes**. While Fillmore was president, he tried to solve the slavery problem. He worked hard to **preserve** the United States.

Outside Buffalo's city hall stands a statue in Fillmore's honor.

Office of the President

Branches of Government

The US government has three branches. They are the executive, legislative, and judicial branches. Each branch has some power over the others. This is called a system of checks and balances.

★ Executive Branch

The executive branch enforces laws. It is made up of the president, the vice president, and the president's cabinet. The president represents the United States around the world. He or she also signs bills into law and leads the military.

★ Legislative Branch

The legislative branch makes laws, maintains the military, and regulates trade. It also has the power to declare war. This branch includes the Senate and the House of Representatives. Together, these two houses form Congress.

★ Judicial Branch

The judicial branch interprets laws. It is made up of district courts, courts of appeals, and the Supreme Court. District courts try cases. Sometimes people disagree with a trial's outcome. Then he or she may appeal. If a court of appeals supports the ruling, a person may appeal to the Supreme Court.

Qualifications for Office

To be president, a candidate must be at least 35 years old. The person must be a natural-born US citizen. He or she must also have lived in the United States for at least 14 years.

Electoral College

The US presidential election is an indirect election. Voters from each state choose electors. These electors represent their state in the Electoral College. Each elector has one electoral vote. Electors cast their vote for the candidate with the highest number of votes from people in their state. A candidate must receive the majority of Electoral College votes to win.

Term of Office

Each president may be elected to two four-year terms. The presidential election is held on the Tuesday after the first Monday in November. The president is sworn in on January 20 of the following year. At that time, he or she takes the oath of office.
It states:

> I do solemnly swear (or affirm) that I will faithfully execute the office of President of the United States, and will to the best of my ability, preserve, protect and defend the Constitution of the United States.

Line of Succession

The Presidential Succession Act of 1947 states who becomes president if the president cannot serve. The vice president is first in the line. Next are the Speaker of the House and the President Pro Tempore of the Senate. It may happen that none of these individuals is able to serve. Then the office falls to the president's cabinet members. They would take office in the order in which each department was created:

Secretary of State

Secretary of the Treasury

Secretary of Defense

Attorney General

Secretary of the Interior

Secretary of Agriculture

Secretary of Commerce

Secretary of Labor

Secretary of Health and Human Services

Secretary of Housing and Urban Development

Secretary of Transportation

Secretary of Energy

Secretary of Education

Secretary of Veterans Affairs

Secretary of Homeland Security

Benefits

★ While in office, the president receives a salary. It is $400,000 per year. He or she lives in the White House. The president also has 24-hour Secret Service protection.

★ The president may travel on a Boeing 747 jet. This special jet is called Air Force One. It can hold 70 passengers. It has kitchens, a dining room, sleeping areas, and more. Air Force One can fly halfway around the world before needing to refuel. It can even refuel in flight!

★ When the president travels by car, he or she uses Cadillac One. It is a Cadillac Deville that has been modified. The car has heavy armor and communications systems. The president may even take Cadillac One along when visiting other countries.

★ The president also travels on a helicopter. It is called Marine One. It may also be taken along when the president visits other countries.

★ Sometimes the president needs to get away with family and friends. Camp David is the official presidential retreat. It is located in Maryland. The US Navy maintains the retreat. The US Marine Corps keeps it secure. The camp offers swimming, tennis, golf, and hiking.

★ When the president leaves office, he or she receives lifetime Secret Service protection. He or she also receives a yearly pension of $203,700. The former president also receives money for office space, supplies, and staff.

33

PRESIDENTS AND THEIR TERMS

PRESIDENT	PARTY	TOOK OFFICE	LEFT OFFICE	TERMS SERVED	VICE PRESIDENT
George Washington	None	April 30, 1789	March 4, 1797	Two	John Adams
John Adams	Federalist	March 4, 1797	March 4, 1801	One	Thomas Jefferson
Thomas Jefferson	Democratic-Republican	March 4, 1801	March 4, 1809	Two	Aaron Burr, George Clinton
James Madison	Democratic-Republican	March 4, 1809	March 4, 1817	Two	George Clinton, Elbridge Gerry
James Monroe	Democratic-Republican	March 4, 1817	March 4, 1825	Two	Daniel D. Tompkins
John Quincy Adams	Democratic-Republican	March 4, 1825	March 4, 1829	One	John C. Calhoun
Andrew Jackson	Democrat	March 4, 1829	March 4, 1837	Two	John C. Calhoun, Martin Van Buren
Martin Van Buren	Democrat	March 4, 1837	March 4, 1841	One	Richard M. Johnson
William H. Harrison	Whig	March 4, 1841	April 4, 1841	Died During First Term	John Tyler
John Tyler	Whig	April 6, 1841	March 4, 1845	Completed Harrison's Term	Office Vacant
James K. Polk	Democrat	March 4, 1845	March 4, 1849	One	George M. Dallas
Zachary Taylor	Whig	March 5, 1849	July 9, 1850	Died During First Term	Millard Fillmore

PRESIDENT	PARTY	TOOK OFFICE	LEFT OFFICE	TERMS SERVED	VICE PRESIDENT
Millard Fillmore	Whig	July 10, 1850	March 4, 1853	Completed Taylor's Term	Office Vacant
Franklin Pierce	Democrat	March 4, 1853	March 4, 1857	One	William R.D. King
James Buchanan	Democrat	March 4, 1857	March 4, 1861	One	John C. Breckinridge
Abraham Lincoln	Republican	March 4, 1861	April 15, 1865	Served One Term, Died During Second Term	Hannibal Hamlin, Andrew Johnson
Andrew Johnson	Democrat	April 15, 1865	March 4, 1869	Completed Lincoln's Second Term	Office Vacant
Ulysses S. Grant	Republican	March 4, 1869	March 4, 1877	Two	Schuyler Colfax, Henry Wilson
Rutherford B. Hayes	Republican	March 3, 1877	March 4, 1881	One	William A. Wheeler
James A. Garfield	Republican	March 4, 1881	September 19, 1881	Died During First Term	Chester Arthur
Chester Arthur	Republican	September 20, 1881	March 4, 1885	Completed Garfield's Term	Office Vacant
Grover Cleveland	Democrat	March 4, 1885	March 4, 1889	One	Thomas A. Hendricks
Benjamin Harrison	Republican	March 4, 1889	March 4, 1893	One	Levi P. Morton
Grover Cleveland	Democrat	March 4, 1893	March 4, 1897	One	Adlai E. Stevenson
William McKinley	Republican	March 4, 1897	September 14, 1901	Served One Term, Died During Second Term	Garret A. Hobart, Theodore Roosevelt

PRESIDENT	PARTY	TOOK OFFICE	LEFT OFFICE	TERMS SERVED	VICE PRESIDENT
Theodore Roosevelt	Republican	September 14, 1901	March 4, 1909	Completed McKinley's Second Term, Served One Term	Office Vacant, Charles Fairbanks
William Taft	Republican	March 4, 1909	March 4, 1913	One	James S. Sherman
Woodrow Wilson	Democrat	March 4, 1913	March 4, 1921	Two	Thomas R. Marshall
Warren G. Harding	Republican	March 4, 1921	August 2, 1923	Died During First Term	Calvin Coolidge
Calvin Coolidge	Republican	August 3, 1923	March 4, 1929	Completed Harding's Term, Served One Term	Office Vacant, Charles Dawes
Herbert Hoover	Republican	March 4, 1929	March 4, 1933	One	Charles Curtis
Franklin D. Roosevelt	Democrat	March 4, 1933	April 12, 1945	Served Three Terms, Died During Fourth Term	John Nance Garner, Henry A. Wallace, Harry S. Truman
Harry S. Truman	Democrat	April 12, 1945	January 20, 1953	Completed Roosevelt's Fourth Term, Served One Term	Office Vacant, Alben Barkley
Dwight D. Eisenhower	Republican	January 20, 1953	January 20, 1961	Two	Richard Nixon
John F. Kennedy	Democrat	January 20, 1961	November 22, 1963	Died During First Term	Lyndon B. Johnson
Lyndon B. Johnson	Democrat	November 22, 1963	January 20, 1969	Completed Kennedy's Term, Served One Term	Office Vacant, Hubert H. Humphrey
Richard Nixon	Republican	January 20, 1969	August 9, 1974	Completed First Term, Resigned During Second Term	Spiro T. Agnew, Gerald Ford

PRESIDENT	PARTY	TOOK OFFICE	LEFT OFFICE	TERMS SERVED	VICE PRESIDENT
Gerald Ford	Republican	August 9, 1974	January 20, 1977	Completed Nixon's Second Term	Nelson A. Rockefeller
Jimmy Carter	Democrat	January 20, 1977	January 20, 1981	One	Walter Mondale
Ronald Reagan	Republican	January 20, 1981	January 20, 1989	Two	George H.W. Bush
George H.W. Bush	Republican	January 20, 1989	January 20, 1993	One	Dan Quayle
Bill Clinton	Democrat	January 20, 1993	January 20, 2001	Two	Al Gore
George W. Bush	Republican	January 20, 2001	January 20, 2009	Two	Dick Cheney
Barack Obama	Democrat	January 20, 2009	January 20, 2017	Two	Joe Biden

"An honorable defeat is better than a dishonorable victory." Millard Fillmore

★ WRITE TO THE PRESIDENT ★

You may write to the president at:
The White House
1600 Pennsylvania Avenue NW
Washington, DC 20500

You may e-mail the president at:
comments@whitehouse.gov

Glossary

American Civil War—the war between the Northern and Southern states from 1861 to 1865.

compromise—an agreement reached after each side gives up something.

debt—something owed to someone else, especially money.

degree—a title given by a college, university, or trade school to its students for completing their studies.

immigrate—to enter into another country to live. A person who immigrates is called an immigrant.

lawyer (LAW-yuhr)—a person who gives people advice on laws or represents them in court.

legislature—a group of people with the power to make or change laws.

nominate—to name as a possible winner.

politics—the art or science of government. Something referring to politics is political. A person who is active in politics is a politician.

preserve—to protect something to keep it in its original state or in good condition.

representative—someone chosen in an election to act or speak for the people who voted for him or her.

resolution—a formal statement of the feelings, wishes, or decision of a group.

running mate—someone running for vice president with another person running for president in an election.

stroke—a medical problem caused by lack of blood flow to the brain. Strokes are serious. They may cause brain damage or death.

support—to believe in or be in favor of something.

telegraph—a machine used to send messages across wires.

threat—something that could be harmful.

treaty—an agreement made between two or more groups.

Whig Party—a US political party active between 1834 and 1854.

★ WEBSITES ★

To learn more about the US Presidents, visit **booklinks.abdopublishing.com**. These links are routinely monitored and updated to provide the most current information available.

39

Index